Barter

. . .

Barter

. . .

Monica Youn

Graywolf Press

Publication of this volume is made possible in part by a grant provided by the Minnesota State Arts Board, through an appropriation by the Minnesota State Legislature; a grant from the Wells Fargo Foundation Minnesota; and a grant from the National Endowment for the Arts. Significant support has also been provided by the Bush Foundation; Marshall Field's Project Imagine with support from the Target Foundation; the McKnight Foundation; and other generous contributions from foundations, corporations, and individuals. To these organizations and individuals we offer our heartfelt thanks.

Special funding for this title has been provided by the Jerome Foundation.

Published by Graywolf Press
250 Third Avenue North, Suite 600
Minneapolis, Minnesota 55401
All rights reserved.

www.graywolfpress.org

Published in the United States of America

ISBN 978-1-55597-381-0

2 4 6 8 9 7 5 3

Library of Congress Control Number: 2002111718

Cover design: Jeenee Lee

Cover art: Elliott Hundley, *Cage* (detail); photographed by Peter Harris

Contents

3

4

the footfalls of a cat
the beards of women
the roots of stones
the breath of fishes
the nerves of bears
the spittle of birds

1

Drawing for Absolute Beginners

Take any desired height, or place points for
top of head and heels. Divide into eighths. . . .

8. Head tilted back between the headboard slats. Eyes glass boxes filling up with light. Later, drained to a blue-gray, the color of good government.

7. Thus, we see that commodification is a function of local necessity.
    a. As Angelenos collect percolating shade in shallow pans, to leach the arsenic out of the light.
    b. "And then I buried it."
    "Where, exactly? And when?"
    "In the chest. Insertion point at the base of the throat. You were still asleep."
    "But what is it, exactly? I mean, I can't figure out its precise extent. I mean, I can feel it there sometimes, like stitches, or sometimes like a flanged or branching bone."

6. Cross-hatchings of street noise and the Minotaur with his boy's body. Narrowing. Rib cage the verge of a canoe. Armpit a whiff of pencil lead.

5. "If you want to fuck me with that bottle, Mr. Arbuckle, best take the foil off first."

4. *osculation*:
    a. The act of kissing. A kiss.
    b. *Math.* A point where two branches of a curve have a common tangent and extend in both directions of the tangent.
    c. To the ankles. Or to the knees. Or just unzipped enough.

3

3. Charmeuse chemise. A shuddering fall. Miss Adelaide Hall on the chaise longue singing *I ain't much caring / Just where I will end.* Then jerked upright, skirt hiked to the knee, that bridge stretching out under every skip-step. Slaphappy scat-puppet of the fixed smile, the meanwhile, *Ain't got nobody to love now.*

2. The bone begging bowl. The foot that pushed it away.

1. "I want to leave you exactly as I found you."

Letter from Contra Costa

Technically edible, like the nasturtiums,
or else softly scoured, or silver-toothed, or shed.

Jadis, my dear, the BART streamed across the bay—
five thousand hosannas, your woodwind spine.

In the streets an air of festival, pumpkin-
colored light sifting through the expatriate trees.

Already you drifting away from me; already your face
rinsed of detail, the inside of an elbow.

Marmoreal meaning white like marble or *marmoreal*
meaning white and hard like marble. I walked

for three hours won't you make the poem Christmas,
the answer to everyone's question, greek fire?

Civil

Cement dust settles on
the raw muscle. "Don't

smutch me.
                    I mean it."

                    . . .

Enter the Queen of Naples
in the guise of Social Virtue.

Enter the lustful
          calling, calling on

          Pasiphaë.

                    . . .

bewitched bewildered

          beware
          beware

I saw you stroking her
coarse red hair. *Honi soit*

(your blue striped collar)
          qui mal y pense

(your blue striped cuff).

25th & Dolores

One could search this landscape in vain
for signs of necessity. From here
the gently tumbled houses,

the tall white hospital, a garland
of palm trees unreeling down the avenue,
and a bright scuffed sky the body

keeps mistaking for grieving.
The calla lilies are one form of life.
How they persist in their slow

unwelling, how they define
luxury as the absence of threat.
"The most beautiful freeway

in America" is beginning
to the right: its heaped-up hills,
its full-strength sunlight burning off

the camphor-infused fog.
You were wrong. I'm still capable
of begging. Crook your arm

around my neck, knees behind
my knees, and march me downhill
into the standing water.

Derivation, *or*
The Unexamined Life

remorse: to be bitten
again. *remonstrance*:

to be displayed again;
shown again; arms

pulled back, head
following, how you

gloat, my reflection
smeared in the midnight

window: *why won't
you look at yourself?*

Fiona Rae

Untitled (white, orange and black), 1995

Thus. A seashell

full of breadcrumbs for an eraser—
room at last for the blush of light

on a white page, all these illicit
Cistercian pleasures. A spiracle,

a breathing hole. Remember when
you were precious, when you wanted to be

impermeable, one among the massed
citizens of the mantelpiece. There.

Bide your time. Comb your hair. It's
brief, but so easy: warm gold oil

drizzled into the willing eye. But always
nearby (in fact, nearer now) the thing

you won't admit to: the thing
with lipstick-colored fur

prowling the boxwood corridors.

After Franz Kline

In what box is it buried—that first
fossilized dawn? What thing in me survived

the sight of you nosing through the bedsheets
for each shed strand of my black hair, before

ten-years-my-elder Allison got home?

Polaroid

found on my windshield 10/13/98

1. *Left*

Flashbulb magnolia
on the lean

brown thigh:
light makes

a peeled thing,
makes a bed

for the eye
to lie in—

yes, to rest
before the work

of learning
more than this

desire so
unforced

(for now)
it blossoms

on the surface
like a salt.

2. *Top Left*

The cock (young
or shaven) and then

this line incised
from root to tip

(fingernail or
butter knife)—

editing that
slight wilt,

demarcating dark
from darker room.

Tilt for a better
view, and watch blue

fingerprints flare
on the emulsion—

fireworks viewed
from far above.

3. *Lower Right*

Then drops
down to that cut-

and-pasted quilt
of cunt. Surely

it should be
blinders, this

splay upon
splay. But can't

keep the eye
from straying

to any detail
not cropped out:

stocking top,
red patent-

leather bow-
tied pump.

4.

Such effort,
young one,

and to what end?
To locate appetite

that would be as
maple in the

mouth? To use
your own hand

to mark the line
between that

darkness and the
encroaching dark?

Titian's *Salome*

stepping out of the sun

pupils expanding as if

dropped in water she

sees all along it had

edges could be stepped

out of a garment or

archway *that light that*

warmth O once beloved

she no longer notices

your hair spilling over

her bare wrist her arm

Ending

Freshwater stunned the beaches. I could sleep.

2

. . .

Stereoscopes

[1]

Oranges
going gelatinous in
the Central Valley as the Dow
neared ten thousand.

[2]

Feathers
spiked with
albumen.

[3]

A piece of cellophane
stretched taut over
her back; dragonflies were
spawning.

[4]

Mayday is
m'aidez.

[5]

What they took
for a star was in fact
a twin star;
their instruments
revealed that
it sometimes was approaching,
sometimes receding.

[6]

The oiled
needle sleeps in its
glossy cradle.

[1]

My love,
I dreamt the wolves
were on you and I was useless
in my open-toed shoes.

[2]

Deodand,
your function
is forfeit.

[3]

An inch-thick sheet of
iron; the moment
you deduce the blowtorch
behind it.

[4]

A trickling
shame.

[5]

A scaffolding
rose out of the floor:
an effigy
of a hanged child
swathed in
bandages, a family tradition
on the tenth birthday.

[6]

How much
we like to imagine
a great wind.

Electronica

amplified hair, breathing, bowls of water, Polish trains
—Matmos, "Schluss"

Felix the Rat's hind feet
could be Barbie hands—
   same pink, same
injection-molded seaming.
Asleep in daylight, his tail
   still disconcerts—
hairless, like that quatrefoil
we found online: a woman part-
   penetrated
front and back (a span of inches),
someone's vision of achieved
   grace, I suppose—
barbiturates and a macro lens.
Meanwhile the kettle ramps
   up to a boil,
stops short, starts over: four
spaced clicks, the gas ignites—
   looped and
digitized. Graphed on-screen,
each soundwave worships
   its neighbors,
seeks its grip on the rhythmic
grid, and must be coaxed
   loose, or
looser—*reverse quantization*,
you explain: to love the world,
   to set soft
baffles in the path of the automatic
architectural—every light that walks
   into this room.

Untropical

Flaky gold all over my
fingertips: peeling

      tangerines.

My purplish scent
discernible around

      your mouth.

Not for you, you
repeat, no hula-

      hoop girl.

Mrs. Caldwell Writes to Her Son

Last night, Eliacim, we attended a special lecture
by an eighteen-year-old lesbian filmmaker
who had given a one-woman show at the Whitney.

She was from Milwaukee
(her watery eyes, the blemishes
on her pale, thick cheeks). There clung to her
something of the breweries: it was as if

her chin and fingertips had been saturated
with the yeasty, exhausted smell of the breweries.

Despite my best intentions, I must admit
my mind drifted. I thought of you,
my love, then found myself recalling

that unfortunate woman at the New Year's Ball
(I'm sure I must have written you) dancing
so vigorously in her boned bodice

before falling completely out of it.
And she kept on—eyes glazed over
mouth gaping open. How rare

an opportunity to witness,
within the space of a few short months,
two separate epiphanies (a word
one has the chance to write
so seldom in the plural).

That unfortunate woman—
the sheen of sweat suddenly cold
on her forehead and upper lip,
as she looked down

and that filmmaker girl—all at once
coarser, more awkward, as she retracted
that earlier statement she had immortalized
with her forty-dollar plastic camera:

"At least I'm not a midget;
at least I'm not a bearded lady."

Three Generations after Larkin

at four A.M., still somewhat dressed,
on my back on a dorm-room floor so coated with wax
you couldn't tell one floorboard from the next;

a boy whose name meant "bookbinder" in Latin,
lips clamped to my collarbone, fast asleep—
how was I to know that only five months hence

he'd come tearing out of the closet;
the night sky brightening
to the same shade of blue

as the Texas flag's star-square
draped over half the window, I wondered
what, if anything, the fuss was all about.

Décor

My covetous eye casts over you,
taking you apart. I'd like a trophy of you
for every room of the house.

The bend of your cocked wrist
in the join of a rafter to the wall;
an eyebrow floated in a cut-glass bowl;

and instead of an antimacassar
draping my overstuffed chair,
a crochet netting of your veins.

Something authoritative,
asymmetrical, perhaps
a bit outré. Featuring that spiral-

shaped mystery of gravitation,
making the room attend it,
composed, aware of distances.

What better in my front hall
with its fan light, its tall
mirrors, than the immaculate

roundness of your plump heel
and toes—substantial, rococo,
a handle for my front door:

warm to the touch,
it turns easily, opens . . . .
You can go now.

Stedelijk

A man in a tight
mesh T-shirt

steps into a huge
gold room and

disappears.
Something flung:

plummet, a plumb
bob. The *Montauk*

woman has not been
given enough skin—

her whole body
is fingers trying

to clench a fist;
downstairs another

woman bleeding
conscientiously

in the shape of a star.
Six centuries ago,

Giotto, the virtuoso,
smirked, and even Cavafy

on his deathbed—shaking
language off his wrist

like a loose
charm bracelet—

learned his lesson
in the end: a circle

inside a circle
suffices for desire.

Hush now, and be
contented. Wait

for the footsteps
to fade. The guard's

wrist-thick braid
is softly swaying;

the chromed stair-
rail hums in tune

with the neverending
harmonized barbershop

croon of the shoulder-
to-shoulder gabled houses.

Stealing *The Scream*

It was hardly a high-tech operation, stealing *The Scream*.
That we know for certain, and what was left behind—
a store-bought ladder, a broken window,
and fifty-one seconds of videotape, abstract as an overture.

And the rest? We don't know. But we can envision
moonlight coming in through the broken window,
casting a bright shape over everything—the paintings,
the floor tiles, the velvet ropes: a single, sharp-edged pattern;

the figure's fixed hysteria rendered suddenly ironic
by the fact of something happening; houses
clapping a thousand shingle hands to shocked cheeks
along the road from Oslo to Asgardstrand;

the guards rushing in—too late!—greeted only
by the gap-toothed smirk of the museum walls;
and dangling from the picture wire like a baited hook,
a postcard: "Thanks for the poor security."

The policemen, lost as tourists, stand whispering
in the galleries: ". . . but what does it all mean?"
Someone has the answers, someone who, grasping the frame,
saw his sun-red face reflected in that familiar boiling sky.

Aneurysm

"All mod cons yet o'erbrimming
with olde worlde charm" might have been your gloss
on the mud-resistant mauve hexagons
of the Normandie Towers, the parfait knight
etched on the glass of the automatic doors.

But you live here now. Irresolute, your white mother,
flown in from Ayrshire, executes a slow twirl—
step-ball-change—holding at arm's length
a trussed-up Douglas fir, shorter than she is,
brought back to the apartment in a cab;

she is amazed
at the enormous refrigerators
of America. I can't help but stare
at the bald, stitched quadrant of your skull
where there had been a fistful of springy hair—

a fistful I saw once, spelunking, belly down
in ammoniac black water, raising my eyes
to where the guide, upright, in standing space,
clutched a flashlit clump of daddy longlegs
off the skittering cave wall: unharmed, excited by the light.

You could raise your eyebrow clear over
the top of your shaved head, but don't.

Water

*The first flying fish first leaped, not because it sought
'adaptation' to the air, but out of horror of the sea.*
—W. B. Yeats, *Autobiographies*

To be thus chastised, thus
set down by some algae-
bearded sea papa
out of Fellini's
Satyricon: "No daughter
of mine" and "Don't
come home again!"

Newly separated fingers
grope for purchase
on the slick cliff wall.
An articulated ankle
trails a salt stream
of droplets, a flash
diamond bracelet.

Labor Day

A glass of tap water that tasted of bruise;
her bronze-stockinged feet overflowed her white shoes.

3

. . .

Verandah

1.

The verandah shooting out
horizontally

across the yard, the deer
fleeing for the trees.

2.

"1,001 Kitchen Miracles."
Something raw in the bread.

3.

The kitty mistook
my forearms for

pigeons and had
to be put down.

4.

That noise you made
was pinkly ludicrous.

5.

She pressed two
fingers behind my ear

until the framed jigsaw
of the black Scottie went

to pieces and I fell.

Alaska Airlines

Like a dolly-mounted
                    death ray,
slow-motion sunlight firing in turn
each inlet, each island lake.

                My tray-table
                Mademoiselle:
                        "Maybe you
                could be a parts model."

Shining delts and pecs:

the mudflats flaunt
their dragon tattoos
                        of water,
one for each lost life.

Alaska Variations

The blue latex of the glacier's glove
on the mountain's furred shoulder,

scrabbled stones on the river path,
a bell to ward off bears. 5 P.M.

The dark drifts down in a fine powder:
fulminate of mercury. October's rust-red

molting salmon seem motionless,
but we know the gray river is moving,

as we know it makes its own noise
under the bear bell's bright

lifesaving chime. Blue "from compression,"
so I'm told, but why compression

should be blue I couldn't
tell you. Axe-heads buried

in the back of a great beast.
Gunpowder trickling

from the mountain's loose fist.
The bear bell hangs a bridle

of bottles over the gravid river.
Blue Gore-Tex windbreaker, bell

strapped to wrist: "Keep moving.
Try to sound as human as you can."

Home Savings

A ridged glass cylinder
(via pneumatic tube)
          hurtles

over six lanes of idling cars,
opens to a slim sheaf of
          twenties,

and, for the holidays,
two starlight
          mints.

A Parking Lot in West Houston

Angels are unthinkable
in hot weather

except in some tropical locales, where
from time to time, the women catch one in their nets,

hang it to dry, and fashion it into a lantern
that will burn forever on its own inexhaustible oils.

But here—shins smocked with heat rash,
the supersaturated air. We no longer believe

in energies pure enough not to carry heat,
nor in connections—the thought of someone

somewhere warming the air we breathe
that one degree more . . . .

In a packed pub during the World Cup final,
a bony redhead woman gripped my arm

too hard. *I could see how a bloke might fancy you.*
Like a child's perfect outline in fast-melting snow,

her wet handprint on my skin, disappearing.
The crowd boiling over, a steam jet: *Brrra-zil!*

And Paris—a heroin addict
who put her hypodermic

to my throat: *Je suis malade.*
J'ai besoin de medicaments.

Grabbing her wrist, I saw
her forearm's tight net sleeve of drying blood.

I don't like to be touched.
I stand in this mammoth parking lot,

car doors open, letting the air conditioner
run for a while before getting in.

The heat presses down equally
everywhere. It wants to focus itself,

to vaporize something instantaneously,
efficiently—that shopping cart, maybe,

or that half-crushed brown-glass bottle—
but can't quite. Asphalt softens in the sun.

Nothing's detachable.
The silvery zigzag line

stitching the tarmac to the sky around the edges
is no breeze, just a trick of heat.

My splayed-out compact car half-sunk
in the tar pit of its own shadow—

strong-shouldered, straining
to lift its vestigial wings.

Night Ferry to Naxos 1

All your carefully cultivated notions of realism

come to an end here, where the sentimental pink
funnels into the Peloponnese

like a rum and grenadine cocktail
poured down a taut throat. Tourist,

this is how the peace drains into you.
Your fingers uncurl on the deck railings,

and over your head, a spiraling umbilical
of ship-smoke loops back to the brown air of Athens,

which only now, behind you, is beginning
to take shape: a smog-shielded dome.

The flattering breeze picks out your contours
in silverpoint—its insinuations

sweet as fresh-laid sheets, a bedtime story,
mother love. Already above you,

half-heard, a tattoo of wingbeats, bare feet
racing in circles on hard-packed dirt.

You will have to become a hero like the rest of us.

Night Ferry to Naxos 2

Another round of *Dona Nobis Pacem*

from the Italian ladies below deck and you know
you'll never be rid of it now.

You're still humming *sotto voce* at 3 A.M.
when the hold's thick wall falls away

to reveal this island, coy as a cameo
on a widow's black bosom.

Since April, a honeyed
habit-forming dew

has been collecting
in the hollows of the rocks,

and the local myths, freshly washed,
have been polishing their bare limbs.

All for you, wind-whipped
and shivering on the gangplank: *deus*

ex machina in silver lamé,
a lobster on an enormous plate, a birth . . . .

Nothing you can do will disappoint them now.

Flatlanders

Here the sky's all spreading belly,
postcoital, pressing the ground
deeper into the ground.

Rumors of incest: a folded
Rorschach, a mirror in love with a lake.

In fenced backyards across Fort Bend County
buttered-up high-school sweethearts
lie on sheets of tinfoil for a tan;

wake up crying, siren-red,
eyelids swollen into temporary lips.

. . .

We know no other shapes
than those that contain us;
we have built our zoneless city,

hub of freeways, a dark étoile.
In Tony's, an ageless lady stirs

her iced tea till the ice cubes melt
to sharp-boned shadows of themselves;
a wink of lime slice, her gem-knuckled hand.

In the garage of St. Joseph's Children's Hospital,
shivering, an intern in short-sleeved scrubs

pulls a soft gold spot into the center
of his cigarette filter, an indrawn breath.

. . .

Hurricane season in the suburbs:
windows asterisked

with masking tape—crosshairs,
false-eyelashed eyes. We remember

when the whole city was a pavé brooch
most of us would covet.

Sometimes we feel lucky:
the hurricane's eye—

our shy neighbors emerge
into the ultramarine
spotlight, the settling leaves,

stand hushed, reverent,
peering up the skirts of the storm.

     . . .

In the eighth grade we learned
a cone pushed through a plane
is a spreading circle to the Flatlanders.

There's no point in looking up.
From time to time a football drops

from the technicolor buzz of stadium lights
into the supplicant hands
of some misshapen archetypal hero.

And on the last night of every year,
the sullen boot-clad men of Pasadena

park on the feeder roads, sit for hours
on the roofs of their pickups,

trying to shoot the fireworks out of the sky.

Venice, Unaccompanied

      Waking
on the train, I thought
we were attacked

      by light:
chrome-winged birds
hatching from the lagoon.

      That first day
the buoys were all
that made the harbor

      bearable:
pennies sewn into a hemline.
Later I learned to live in it,

      to walk
through the alien city—
a beekeeper's habit—

      with fierce light
clinging to my head and hands.
Treated as gently as every

      other guest—
each house's barbed antennae
trawling for any kind

      of weather—
still I sobbed in a glass box
on an unswept street

with the last
few lire ticking like fleas
off my phonecard *I'm sorry*

    I can't
stand this, which
one of us do you love?

Hand to Mouth

the fields flooded with milk
the herbs shining on the mountain

the strong   salt soil   my dear

you stoop to pinch off eatings

while behind you a vast
task is rising
               a skein of use

Kestrel: Etymology

a *groom*, a *varlet*—one pressed into use:
a gymnast trembling in his Iron Cross.

4

...

Muscae Volitantes

The train lights dimmed again:
dead spots along the Northeast Line.

The conductor wished aloud for
an insulated hand to smooth them.

   . . .

a cellophane glove
a silvertone stave

   . . .

"It's still there. It was
a planet, not a plane."

   . . .

a muttering hive
a travertine nave

   . . .

The single strand
radio tower.

Three empty crystal
biscuit barrels.

   . . .

a blustering grove
a listening cave

   . . .

"But, oh my poor Mathilde,
mine was only paste!"

   . . .

a bustling dove
a ritalin rave

. . .

There was middle
C and there was high

C and no other
C could come between them.

. . .

a porcelain sieve
an oxygen grave

. . .

". . . to which I cannot
bring myself to aspire."

. . .

a clementine love
a glycerine wave

Doe

in headlights in the Marin headlands:
hind legs lit for an instant, tapering, taupe,

on tiptoe—the half-mannequin hosiery display
at Dillard's I could watch for hours, hidden

in a toroid rack of satin half-slips,
hoarding price tags I thought were receipts.

St. Benedict's Painted Church

Honaunau, Kona

Something, a fruit perhaps,
or a bowl of fruit—
something collapsed

in upon itself,
collapsed in on itself
again and again till it rose

in packed banks, layer
upon layer, a carnival-
colored amphitheater.

But it can't have been like that,
as I remembered it. I've lost
both postcards,

my notebook: *a man upright*
in the tomb rays of light
threaded through his palms

a sainted marionette . . .
the fig tree trunks
are spiraling scrolls

spiraling praise him . . . .
No, it would be better to start
from the beginning, the outside:

a green hill rising
out of an island
rising out of the sea.

Then nearer, it is peaked,
foursquare: the marvelous
origami husband-

hunting machines
we folded out of hymn sheets
during Children's Mass—

shuffling once, twice,
forty times, then lifting a flap
to reveal a name.

And finally, so dramatically
the gravel bursts into applause
as we skid to a stop on the driveway,

it's there: clapboarded, so much
in earnest, the sunlight
hung out to dry on its pitched roof.

We step inside, into that shaped
impenetrable space *as if
a seed had sprouted*

while still inside the shell.
Louder outside the slow ticking
of the actual vegetation.

Fort Tryon Park

Itch of squirrels
　　　　in the dry leaves:
should I have worn

　　　　　my warmer coat?
Mortared and
　　　　bordered, switch-

backs and oxbows:
　　　　how one's descents
must be measured;

　　　　how I once
woke to find
　　　　all physical

courage gone.
　　　　The blind-white
wipe of Hudson,

　　　　the GW Bridge
suspension tower's
　　　　slats of sunset light

call to mind
　　　　my Helena's wired jaw
when she spent winter

　　　　sipping sustenance
through a flattened
　　　　pink straw.

Käthe Kollwitz

Death, Woman and Child

at last our two faces smeared into one
distorted, shiny in this new bliss;

one thin arm: a high rolled collar
circling our conjoined neck.

The Scythian Lamb

1.

How was myopic Sir John
of Mandeville to know
that what he glimpsed on the far bank

of the monsoon-fed Kabul
was but a hapless woolly fern,
tossed, fronds down, roots up,

by a badger in pursuit
of a frantic, wide-eyed
white-footed mouse.

It grew dark early at that time of year,
and, too, his reading public
were hungry for more living logs,

river horses, and rabbits in plate armor
with the faces of Christian martyrs—
anything to keep their minds

off the Black Death.
The travelers stopped, made camp.
Sir John shook out his pen.

"In the wilds of Scythia,"
he wrote, "there grows
a wondrous and woolly thing

half-beast, half-vegetable,
a lambkin on a stalk."
He paused, looked out again

over the darkening
Afghan river. "Its cloven hooves
cannot reach ground;

for sustenance, it munches
those grasses within its reach."
Sir John moved closer to the fire.

"When this fails, as it must,
the Scythian lamb will wither.
The wind carries its seeds

to more fertile soil, leaving only
a dried-up stalk, a circle
of close-cropped earth."

2.

In February, in Fort Worth
before the nightly news,
ten-year-old Douglas Hill

tried not to make a sound
as he went down the basement stairs
to get a beer for his father.

He tiptoed across the concrete floor
toward the refrigerator,
averting his eyes from the opposite wall

where his older brother Stephen
(now at sixty pounds)
sat chained to a pipe in the corner.

Douglas risked a look back . . .
then grabbed the beer and ran,
footsteps thudding up the stairs,

the refrigerator slamming shut,
as he tried to clear his mind
of the sight of his brother:

dull-eyed, quiescent,
jaws working methodically
on a mouthful that wasn't there.

10 Years Old

She came to understand death
    early. Her friend Sue
        had a birthmark:

bordered, brown,
    the size of a coin.
        A stillness pooled there

and in the concave
    tension of the backs of her hands.
        Her mouth a white ridge

(sewn shut, smoothed over)
    when they buried her.
        She thought, then, that it was gone,

but opening her presents
    that year, she felt it again—
        a slight fluttering

of skin and muscles around
    that same stillness
        at the center: weightless,

the size of her two fists.
    And it was inside her—
        escaping, hollowing out

her legs, each separate
    finger, scraping up against
        the underside of her skin.

(For a long time she searched
       the mirror each morning
              for signs of leakage.)

She had been learning,
       then, to speak clearly—
              each syllable certain

as if dipped in glass;
       and she knew
              she was a container

for something else,
       and movement
              just a scurrying

across the surface.

103 Korean Martyrs

Where was it that we went that night?
That long, low building: floodlights
rimmed in lavender, the moon ringed
in rose. I would rather, then, have stayed

outside, where spiderwebs glowed
like jellyfish in the damp yew hedges,
where the paths were chalky pebbles
set with giant stepping stones.

But the film was starting. In the air-
conditioned dark, a crowd of strangers,
strange families (not from our church)
in rows of metal folding chairs to see

a man quartered by horses: strain
stitched across his shining back
then, all over at once, an unraveling
and then the spill of meat;

a girl pushed through a doorway,
naked among the soldiers:
she grew a dress to cover herself,
a blue dress with a blinding sash.

Flowerbed

Consummately demure

    white bouquets
     of alyssum:

     are they
   sufficiently

the "irresistible flower"

   of my story?

    . . .

Dig a hole with your hands, she will live there.

With a wax paper roof, she will thrive there.

And a pine needle bed, she'll behave there.

Block the entrance with dirt, she won't leave there.

Naglfar

she said   they are building the ship
the color of steam   the color of salt

the end of the world   she stopped
speaking   she was alone

she spent hours   cutting her fingernails
they won't take them   when I die

she said   for the ridged sides
of their ship   cutting off

the white crescents   they looked
like tiny boats   they collected

in her pockets   in the seams of her dress
I am trying   she said

holding out   her nailless hands
to prevent   the end of the world

Ragnarok   she said
if startled   her eyes strayed

to the notched petals of the dogwoods
the flecks of mica in the path

Notes

The book's epigraph is taken from the Norse myth of the ribbon Gleipnir, which is made of nonexistent things, or things taken out of the world for this purpose. The ribbon was intended to bind Fenris Wolf until the battle at the end of the world, Ragnarok.

The epigraph for **Drawing for Absolute Beginners** comes from illustrator Andrew Loomis's 1943 book *Figure Drawing for All It's Worth*, where he explains the "eight heads" model of the ideal male proportion. The eight divisions are: (8) top of head to chin, (7) chin to nipples, (6) nipples to navel, (5) navel to crotch, (4) crotch to midthigh, (3) midthigh to knee, (2) knee to midcalf, and (1) midcalf to heel.

In **Civil**, the Queen of Naples is a character in Proust who saves the Baron de Charlus from humiliation by offering him her arm. The lustful and their cries to Pasiphaë occur in Canto XXVI of the *Purgatorio*. The sentence *Honi soit qui mal y pense* ("Shame be on him who thinks ill of this") is the motto of the Order of the Garter, founded by Edward III in 1348. At a feast in 1347, the king's mistress, the Countess of Salisbury, was mocked for losing her garter during a dance, but Edward at once stepped forward and tied the blue ribbon around his own knee, uttering the motto as a rebuke and declaring that the Garter would soon be held in the highest esteem.

Electronica is for Drew Daniel and Martin Schmidt, a.k.a. Matmos. The epigraph is from the liner notes to their eponymous first album (Vague Terrain, 1997). The notes list the ingredients used to make the track.

Mrs. Caldwell Writes to Her Son is based on Camilo José Cela's *Mrs. Caldwell Speaks to Her Son* (J.S. Bernstein, trans., Cornell University Press, 1968).

The **Stedelijk** ("Municipal") Museum in Amsterdam's de Kooning collection includes the painting *Montauk IV*. According to an anecdote in Vasari's *The Lives of the Artists*, Giotto, asked to submit a drawing for a papal commission, won the competition by simply painting a perfect circle freehand. Cavafy's last motion was to draw a circle on a blank sheet of paper and then place a period in the middle of the circle.

Stealing *The Scream* is based on the painting's February 1994 theft.

Alaska Airlines: The mudflats surrounding Anchorage have claimed lives when walkers have gotten stuck in quicksand and the bore tides have come roaring in, covering the mudflats in up to thirty feet of water.

Night Ferry to Naxos 1: As part of the ancient Greek cults of hero worship, some heroes were buried in graves that featured a funnel opening at surface level that led down into the hero's mouth. Suppliants could pour blood down the funnel in order to get the dead hero to speak.

Mandeville refers to **The Scythian Lamb** in his account of the land of "Cadhilhe" (possibly Korea). My *OED* dismisses the Scythian Lamb or barometz as "a spurious natural-history specimen, consisting of the creeping root-stock and frond-stocks of a woolly fern (*Cibotium barometz*); formerly represented as a creature half animal and half plant." In one of the most widely publicized child abuse cases in recent years, thirteen-year-old Stephen Hill was chained to a metal bar in his parents' trailer home and starved to death. When investigators discovered him in a coma, he weighed fifty-five pounds. He died of a heart attack and blood poisoning twelve days later.

10 Years Old is dedicated to the memory of Theresa Soo-Hyun Kim.

103 Korean Martyrs: Between 1863 and 1876 in the Choson Dynasty, 103 Korean Catholics were martyred when a xenophobic prince regent blamed Korea's problems on foreign influences.

Naglfar (literally, "Ship of Nails") was the Ship of the Dead in Norse mythology. In the underworld, the dead were building a ship made of the uncut fingernails of the dead. The completion of this ship would be one of the signs that the twilight of the gods was at hand. Thus, apparently, the ancient Norse would cut off the fingernails of the dead before burial, hoping, in this way, to delay the onset of the end of the world.

Acknowledgments

Thanks are due to the editors of the following journals in which some of these poems first appeared: *AGNI, American Letters & Commentary, Chelsea, Denver Quarterly, Explosive, Fence, New England Review, Oxford Poetry, PN Review, Poetry Review, Provincetown Arts,* and *Thumbscrew.* Additionally, some of these poems have been included in the anthologies *Asian American Poetry: The Next Generation* (University of Illinois Press, 2003) and *New Poetries II* (Carcanet Press, 1999).

Thanks to the Rhodes Scholarship Trust, the Wallace Stegner Fellowship, and the Corporation of Yaddo for buying me time.

Finally, love to my family and friends, especially those who helped with this manuscript: Rick Barot, Jessica Bennett, Steve Burt, Drew Daniel, Simone Di Piero, Katy Lederer, Jon Leidecker, Claudia Rankine, Martin Schmidt, Mark Wunderlich, and Jason Zuzga.

MONICA YOUN is the author of *Barter* (Graywolf Press, 2003) and *Ignatz* (Four Way Books, 2010), which was a finalist for the National Book Award in Poetry. She lives in Manhattan.

Barter has been set in Berkeley, which is a revision of Frederic Goudy's 1938 University of California Oldstyle. The ITC version was drawn by Tony Stan and issued in 1983.

Book design by Wendy Holdman
Typesetting by Bookmobile Design & Digital Publisher Services
Manufactured by Bookmobile on acid-free paper